759

This book is due for return on or before the last date shown below.

Directions In Art

Painting

Richard Stemp

Heinemann
LIBRARY

H www.heinemann.co.uk/library

Visit our website to find out more information about Heinemann Library books.

To order:
☎ Phone 44 (0) 1865 888066
▤ Send a fax to 44 (0) 1865 314091
▯ Visit the Heinemann Bookshop at www.heinemann.co.uk/library to browse our catalogue and order online.

First published in Great Britain by Heinemann Library, Halley Court, Jordan Hill, Oxford OX2 8EJ, part of Harcourt Education. Heinemann is a registered trademark of Harcourt Education Ltd.

Editorial: Lucy Thunder and Helen Cannons
Design: Jo Hinton-Malivoire and AMR
Picture Research: Hannah Taylor and Elaine Willis
Production: Edward Moore

Originated by Ambassador Litho Ltd
Printed and bound in China by South China Printing Company

ISBN 0 431 17643 4
07 06 05 04 03
10 9 8 7 6 5 4 3 2 1

British Library Cataloguing in Publication Data
Stemp, Richard
Painting. – (Directions in art)
759
A full catalogue record for this book is available from the British Library.

Acknowledgements
The Publishers would like to thank the following for permission to reproduce photographs: The Artist / Courtesy of Marlborough Fine Art, London p**45**; The Artist / The National Gallery, London p**46**; Collection of the artist / National Gallery of Art, Washington, D.C. p**7**; Michael Craig-Martin / Manchester Art Gallery p**15**; Michael Craig-Martin / Manchester Art Gallery (John Davies) pp**13**, **14**; Lucien Freud / Private Collection p**17**; Lucian Freud / Tate, London 2003 p**18**; Howard Hodgkin / Tate London 2003 p**25**; Alana Jelinek pp**29**, **30**, **31**; Modern Art Museum of Fort Worth p**27**; The National Gallery, London p**47**; Ana Maria Pacheco / Pratt Contemporary Art p**38**; Ana Maria Pacheco / Pratt Contemporary Art / The National Gallery, London p**37**; Photo RMN / Succession Picasso / DACS 2003 p**5**; Jackson Pollock / Stedelijk Museum Amsterdam / ARS, NY and DACS, London 2003 p**41**; Private Collection, James Goodman Gallery New York / Bridgeman Art Library / ADAGP, Paris and DACS, London 2003 p**10**; Rex Features / Martha Holmes / Timepix p**42**; Bridget Riley pp**48**, **49**; Tate, London 2003 pp**33**, **34**, **35**; Tate, London 2003 / David Hockney pp**21**, **23**; Topham Picturepoint p**9**.

Cover photograph of *Joseph's Dream* by Paula Rego (1990) reproduced with permission of The Artist / Courtesy of Marlborough Fine Art, London.

The Publishers would like to thank Emma Nicolson, Senior Education Officer, and Frances Fowle, Curator, at the National Galleries of Scotland for their assistance in the preparation of this book.

CONTENTS

Any words appearing in the text in bold, **like this**, are explained in the Glossary.

DIRECTIONS IN PAINTING

As long ago as 1435 an Italian writer called Alberti wrote that when he painted he started by drawing a rectangle, 'which is considered to be an open window through which I see what I want to paint'. For many artists through the following centuries this is what painting was. The picture frame became like a window on to the world, which they attempted to paint as realistically as possible.

In Alberti's time the main reason to paint was to decorate churches with stories from the Bible and the lives of Saints. His writing was part of the **Renaissance**, when art and artists became far more important than they had been. As well as religious paintings, artists started to illustrate stories from classical mythology, and new types of painting – such as portraiture and landscape – were developed.

What is a painting?

The surface an artist paints on is known as the support. Although wooden panels were used regularly up until the 17th century, by the end of the 15th century most artists chose to paint on canvas. The cloth is pulled tight around a frame or **stretcher** and attached with nails or staples. The support needs to be sealed before painting, otherwise the paint will soak into it. This is done with a type of glue, called size.

All paints have two components, the **pigments**, or colours, and the **medium**. The medium is a liquid mixed with the pigment, which lets you paint with it. In Alberti's time the most common paint was called **tempera** – the medium was egg yolk. During the 15th century artists started to use oil paint: the pigment is mixed with oil – usually linseed oil.

Changing ideas

In the second half of the 19th century artists' attitudes towards painting changed dramatically. After the invention of photography, it became less important to paint the world exactly as we see it. The **Impressionists** developed a style, which at the time was thought of as sketchy and unfinished. Their atmospheric paintings evoking a mood or feeling of a place are very popular today. A new type of paintbrush had been introduced – flat rather than round – and the paint could be applied in broad brush strokes. These brush strokes were visible on the finished painting: you could see how the painting had been made. In the 20th century the brush strokes themselves, and the different ways marks could be made, became one of the things that paintings were about.

Towards abstract painting

Mark making is certainly an important feature of **Cubism**, a style of painting developed by Pablo Picasso (1881–1973) and Georges Braque (1882–1963) from about 1907. Rather than a simple depiction, Cubists analyse and interpret what they are looking at, as if they are moving around the subject, showing different parts of it from different points of view. For example, in *Still Life with Chair-Caning* the base of the glass looks more or less circular, as if you are looking down on it. The stem and the overlapping lines, which make up its sides, are vertical, as if you are looking at it from the side.

However fragmented Cubist paintings may appear, they are always **representational** – they are paintings of something. In the decade from 1910 to 1920 artists such as Kandinsky (1866–1944) and Piet Mondrian (1872–1944) gradually stopped painting 'things' to concentrate on building up **abstract** images based on colour, line, texture and pattern.

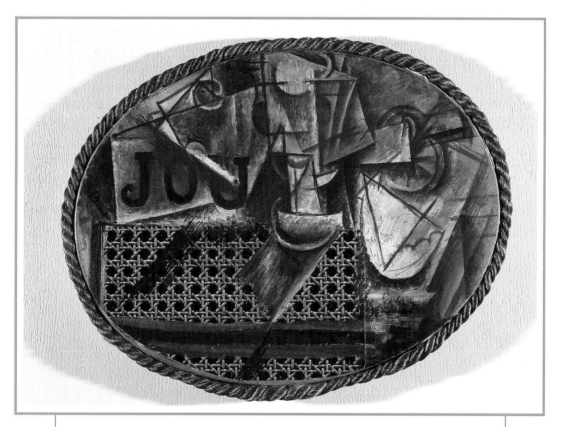

Picasso, Still Life with Chair-Caning *(1912), Musee Picasso, Paris. As well as oil paint, Picasso has used real objects in the picture: a cloth printed to look like chair-caning and a length of rope to frame the image.*

Pablo Picasso

Picasso was born in Spain in 1881. He was the son of an artist, who taught him to paint from the age of ten. He held his first exhibition in 1900, and the following year he moved to Paris, which at the time was considered to be the centre of the art world.

His style of painting changed rapidly. Having developed Cubism, in 1911 he started to use new materials – the *Still Life with Chair-Caning* includes a piece of cloth printed to look like chair-caning, and is framed by real rope. By introducing new materials Picasso opened up the possibilities of painting. He regularly changed his style and technique, and the richness and variety of his work made him one of the most influential artists of the 20th century.

Different movements

The **Surrealists**, who became important in the 1920s, were not interested in abstraction, although the strange combinations of imagery made their work seem dreamlike and unreal. Nevertheless, their interest in the **subconscious** mind was influential in the 1940s for Abstract Expressionism, an American movement whose artists used their own feelings and subconscious gestures as the starting point for abstract paintings.

One of the Abstract Expressionists, Jackson Pollock (see pages 40–43), was responsible for an important change in painting technique when he stopped using brushes and started dripping and pouring paint directly on to the canvas. Another American, Helen Frankenthaler (b.1928), took this idea further by pouring paint on to **un-sized** canvasses. Without the sealing layer, the paint soaked into the canvas and stained it – this technique became more practical with the development of **acrylic** paints, which can be made more fluid than oils.

What is painting now?

By the beginning of the 21st century painting can take many forms and have many functions, as you will see from the artists we will examine in this book. It can be abstract or representational, purely about appearance or with a message. For Howard Hodgkin it is important to see the way the paint is applied (see pages 24–27), whereas Bridget Riley makes sure that the brush strokes are not visible (see pages 48–49). Artists can use any variety of paints, materials and means of applying them – whereas Jackson Pollock developed new techniques, Ana Maria Pacheco is inspired by traditional methods (see pages 36–39).

Paintings use a wide range of supports and are displayed in many different settings: Michael Craig-Martin's work (see pages 12–15) is painted on the wall, and takes up an entire room. Chris Ofili (see pages 32–35) leans his paintings against the wall, while Alana Jelinek's (see pages 28–31) lie on the floor or belong outside. The artists in this book have been chosen to illustrate the diversity of modern painting and show that, if you know what you are doing, painting can be almost anything you like.

Helen Frankenthaler, Mountains and Sea, 1952, National Gallery of Art, Washington. Unlike many of her contemporaries, Helen Frankenthaler's work always contains a representational aspect, as the title suggests.

JEAN-MICHEL BASQUIAT

In his lifetime Jean-Michel Basquiat was both celebrated as a genuine success and put down as the product of media hype. He became successful relatively young, having his first one-man show in Italy in 1981 at the age of 21. Seven years later a promising career was cut short when he died of a drug overdose.

Basquiat was born into a middle-class family in Brooklyn, New York in 1960. His father was an accountant from Haiti and his mother, of African and Puerto Rican descent, would regularly take him to museums and show him the paintings. At the age of six he became a 'Junior Member' of the Brooklyn Museum.

Despite a good upbringing and an early introduction to art, when Basquiat became famous it was as a wild child from the streets. He had left home at the age of seventeen and lived rough in abandoned buildings. Together with a friend he invented a character called 'SAMO' whose name was applied to slogans written on the walls and subways of downtown Manhattan – precisely the areas where artists and art dealers would see them.

Outsider or mainstream?

Basquiat was picked up by the art establishment as a maker of **Graffiti Art**, a trend that reached its height in the late 1970s. Cynics said that the art dealers and collectors who sought his work were out to look for the 'real thing', a genuine black kid from the streets. If this was what they had in mind, it was an attitude that Basquiat was opposed to, saying, 'I don't know if my being black has anything to do with my success. I don't think I should be compared to black artists, but with all artists.' He really wanted to be considered part of the mainstream art world rather than as the product of a subculture. His work was strongly influenced by a number of contemporary artists, and he certainly never wanted to be thought of as a Graffiti Artist. Even though Basquiat's early slogans were written on walls, they were purely verbal and did not have the decorative quality and rich colours of Graffiti Art.

> *I start with a picture and then finish it. I don't think about art when I'm working. I try to think about life.* JEAN-MICHEL BASQUIAT

Influences

Basquiat was influenced by the simplicity of children's art – something he shares in common with the French artist Jean Dubuffet (1901–85). It was for this direct, apparently uneducated approach that artists like Picasso, another of Basquiat's influences, had valued the masks of so-called **primitive** cultures. As Basquiat became more conscious of his own ancestry, he also drew on the imagery of African tribal masks.

His interest in the human figure was inspired by an anatomy book his mother had given him as a child, and he was fascinated by the anatomical drawings of **Renaissance** artist Leonardo da Vinci (1452–1519). Among contemporary artists, he particularly liked Cy Twombly (b. 1928), whose work – like Basquiat's – explores a combination of **painterly** and **graphic** effects. His admiration for pop artist Andy Warhol (1928–87) led to them becoming friends, and they even made paintings together.

Arroz con Pollo

The title of this painting, *Arroz con Pollo* (1981), translates from the Spanish as 'Rice with Chicken'. As a child, Basquiat spoke with his mother in Spanish – she was half Puerto Rican – and Spanish references were common in his early works. The painting shows two figures, a skeleton-like man on the right and a more solid looking woman on the left. In between them is a grill or barbecue with flames bursting out of it, and the man is handing the woman a roast chicken. The depiction of people – specifically black people – was a constant theme of Basquiat's work. His characters are often given special status by the addition of a spiky halo or crown of thorns, as the man is here.

Basquiat built-up his imagery through a combination of painting and drawing. The outlines of the figures and signs and symbols in the background could be described as graphic, while the broad areas of bright colour are far more painterly. Apart from the carefully drawn and painted chicken most of the imagery is simplistic and sketchy. This gives *Arroz con Pollo* an unsophisticated feel like the paintings of young children – a comparison Basquiat was happy to accept, saying, 'I like kids' work more than work by real artists any day.'

Technique

Basquiat did not prepare his paintings – his approach was spontaneous, and he allowed the paintings to evolve gradually. He would often start by painting a background colour – he usually used **acrylics** – and outlined the main figures with oilstick (effectively paint in the form of a crayon). These would then be coloured in, and changed, with different details being drawn and painted on top of one another until Basquiat was happy that the painting was finished.

In *Arroz con Pollo* one of the early layers was black, with white markings on it: a section of this layer can still be seen towards the top left corner of the painting. This was covered by a layer of red-pink paint varying in intensity across the canvas. The two figures were drawn on top of this with black oilstick. A rich golden-yellow layer was added, covering the figure on the left, which then had to be redrawn – the spiky hair of the original version can just be seen through the yellow paint and sticking out above it. The steaming chicken was painted over an extra white layer, which helps to make it stand out.

Sold short?

Basquiat's first art dealer, Annina Nosei, allowed him to work in the basement of her gallery, providing all the materials he needed. He would often work on more than one painting at a time, gradually building up layers of different ideas. One of the problems of working in Nosei's basement was that collectors were so keen to buy Basquiat's work that she would sell paintings that had not even been finished.

MICHAEL CRAIG-MARTIN

Michael Craig-Martin's earliest work was as a sculptor, but he made his name creating **Conceptual** Art – art in which the idea behind the work can be more important than what you actually see. His work gradually moved towards a form of painting in which looking, and the act of seeing, became of vital importance.

> *I want my work to produce a sense of wonder and pleasure. I want someone to walk into the room and be knocked out by it, to be amazed by what they see.* MICHAEL CRAIG-MARTIN

Craig-Martin was born in Dublin, Ireland in 1941, but went to the United States with his family at the age of four. Having studied Art at Yale University, he moved to Britain in 1966, where he has lived ever since. As well as making his own work, he teaches at Goldsmiths College in London, where he has had a huge influence on the younger generation of artists, including Damien Hirst and Julian Opie.

Inhale/Exhale

Inhale/Exhale (2002) was created for the reopening of Manchester Art Gallery, UK, in May 2002, and was on view there for just over a month. The work took up an entire room in the museum's new extension, and as such can be described as an **installation**. Walking into the space the first impression was of a medley of bright and exciting colours.

Three of the walls of the room did not have any doors – they were all painted magenta – a rich, deep-pink. The fourth wall had two doors, and in between them an area of the wall, marked off by an architectural structure, was painted a bright, acid-green. The structure of the work was clearly decided by the structure of the room – it was **site specific**.

An unframed painting of a collection of objects packed closely together was hung on the green section. The images were clear and easily identifiable – they included a pencil sharpener, a globe, a tape cassette and a metronome (which is used to give the right speed for a piece of music) – but the colours were bright and non-naturalistic. The simple line drawings were not to scale – the light bulb was far bigger than the globe, for example. The background colour of the painting was hard to see, as it was so crowded, but it was actually the same magenta as used for the other three walls.

Opposite the painting, on the main magenta wall, were images of the same objects that were painted on the canvas. They appeared to spread out from the centre of the wall. A few wrapped around on to the side walls, as if they had flown out from the canvas to the other side of the room. It was as if they had been breathed in to the painting – inhaled – and then breathed out again on to the opposite wall – exhaled – which explains the title.

The only object that was not in the painting appeared in front of the globe in the middle of the wall. It was, in fact, a picture of the back of the painting itself – you could see the **stretcher** as a yellow frame. But as the canvas was painted a pale blue, it could almost have been a window – a bit like the imaginary window mentioned by Alberti (see page 4).

Inhale/Exhale – *the canvas hung on the green section of the wall shows all the objects painted on the other walls. It is as if the objects, and the canvas have settled here before being blown across to the other side of the room.*

Meaning

Craig-Martin has been using similar images for over twenty years, and some of the objects he uses have specific meanings. The globe represents the world, but if the canvas is 'a window on the world', it seems to get in the way. The globe can be seen more clearly in the painting on the opposite wall; perhaps art is one of the best ways of seeing the world. The artist has said that the installation 'is an exercise about the nature of painting, about the relationship of painting to the world.'

The other objects were in pairs on the wall. The light bulb and metronome could represent qualities such as light and time, for example, while the book and cassette may stand for literature and music. However, Craig-Martin allows us to connect these objects and their possible meanings in any way we choose: 'There's no sustained symbolism, but sometimes objects seem too obviously symbolic. These are leads that take you so far, but don't ever fully account for things. It's really up to you to make of things what you will.'

Michael Craig-Martin sticking tape over the line drawings that are being projected by slide on to the wall.

Technique

It took four days to install *Inhale/Exhale*, but that was just the actual making of the piece. In order to install it this quickly, everything had to be planned in advance. Designs were drawn up, slides made of the objects, and the canvas painting was completed in the artist's studio in London.

Before Craig-Martin and his assistants started working on site, the walls of the room had already been painted. The slides of the outline drawings of the objects were projected on to the walls. Black tape was then stuck over the projection to transfer the drawings on to the wall. All the area within the tape was then painted white, to neutralize the background colour, and the final colours painted over this. A second layer of tape was then stuck down over the first to cover the joins between the colours and to give the objects their crisp outline.

Influences

In his early work Craig-Martin showed a clear interest in 20th century artists, such as Marcel Duchamp (1887–1968), whose creation of the **readymade** was one of the innovations which led to Conceptual Art. He has also been influenced by artists from the 14th and 15th centuries, saying that, 'I am interested in a lot of pre-20th century art, but in general I prefer early Italian **Renaissance** artists like Giotto and Piero della Francesca. At that time artists needed a certain simplicity and clarity so that their audience would get the point immediately, and key images, signs, gestures and **narratives** were commonly used.'

LUCIAN FREUD

As long ago as 1987 the art critic Robert Hughes said that 'Lucian Freud has become the greatest living realist painter', a position which many people think was confirmed by a large-scale exhibition of his work at Tate Britain, London in 2002.

Freud was born in Berlin in 1922, only moving to England with his family in 1933 as a result of the worsening political situation in Germany and the rise to power of Adolf Hitler. Although he went to the Central School of Art in London, the teaching methods did not suit him and he left after only a term, going on to the East Anglian School of Drawing and Painting.

Even after World War II, when Freud's career started to take off, life in England was not easy. Rationing continued, and a sense of anxiety remained. This mood seems to have affected Freud's paintings ever since. His human subjects, whether painted on their own, or with others, often look lonely, isolated or simply worried.

Patience and concentration

It can take a long time for Freud to finish a painting – around nine months is not uncommon – and the sitter will visit his studio three or four times a week during that time. Each sitting can last up to seven hours, and require as much patience from the subject as it does concentration from Freud himself.

Other subjects

Freud does not just paint people and animals. Works such as *Factory in North London* (1972) are painted with the same close attention to detail. The textures of the brick and plaster are carefully varied, there is the contrast of the horizontals of the building, the verticals of the pipe work and the diagonals of the staircase, and Freud has investigated the individuality of every window. Across the front of the painting a brick wall with sharp, broken glass fragments keeps us away, giving the factory a similar distanced and unapproachable character that we can see in a lot of Freud's human subjects.

> *What do I ask of a painting? I ask it to astonish, disturb, seduce, convince.* LUCIAN FREUD

Factory in North London, *1972. Freud moved to Paddington in north-west London in 1943 – by the time he painted this factory 29 years later it was as familiar to him as the faces of some of his human subjects.*

Influences

Freud claims to have been inspired more by French art than the German artists who were working during his childhood. According to him this is simply, 'Because it happens to be better.' He is interested in the work of Jean-Auguste-Dominique Ingres (1780–1867), one of the great portrait painters, and of Jean Baptiste Siméon Chardin (1699–1779).

Double Portrait

The characters in *Double Portrait* (1985–86) – a girl and a dog – appear to be more at ease with themselves than some of Freud's subjects, who tend to convey loneliness or anxiety. The stillness, which is a common feature of his work, is enhanced by a feeling of comfort, a result of the way in which the two figures are resting on top of one another. Their heads, legs and arms are intertwined, and the dog's snout is resting on the girl's hand.

The relaxed feeling is also supported by the colouration. Freud uses a limited **palette**, which helps to create a harmonious feeling. The grey of the girl's dress is **stippled** onto the wall behind her, and is seen in the opening of the doorway at the top left, as well as in the darker areas of the dog's fur. The creams and whites of the dog's fur are continued through the girl's flesh, and into the wall at the top right.

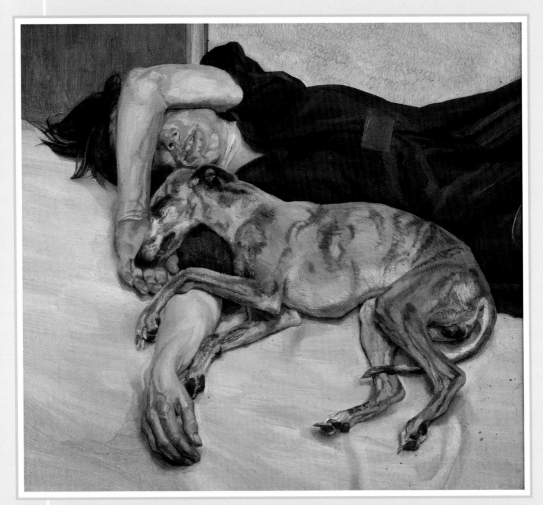

Composition

The **composition** is the way in which the elements of the painting have been arranged, and takes into account the shape and proportions of the painting itself. In *Double Portrait* Freud has clearly fitted the composition to the shape of the canvas. The girl's left arm, bent in a right angle at the elbow, neatly matches the top left hand corner of the painting. The forearm is parallel to the vertical of the door frame, and to her other arm. Against the straight lines of the limbs, the bodies form a series of overlapping and echoing curves – compare the shape of the dog's back to the curve of the girl's body against the wall, for example.

Technique

Although Freud has painted with oil on canvas for the majority of his career, his style of painting changed dramatically in the 1950s when he changed his materials. His earlier paintings were quite **graphic** – they relied a lot on line, and the paint looks fairly thin and flat. But during the fifties Freud changed the type of brush he was using, from **sable** to hogshair (pig's hair). As a result his paintings have become less graphic and more **painterly** – the paint is thicker, and there seems to be a greater enjoyment of the paint itself and the way in which it is applied.

Freud has also experimented with different types of paint. In the mid-seventies he started using a lead-based paint called cremnitz white, which is so thick and dense that it sticks out of the painting, a technique known as **impasto**. He often uses this in the fleshier parts of his paintings, which he builds-up layer by layer. This is most noticeable in *Double Portrait* in the two figures' faces made up of short brush strokes in a variety of colours – pinks, ochres, greens and yellows.

> *As far as I am concerned the paint is the person. I want it to work for me just as flesh does.* LUCIAN FREUD

Different types of brush stroke define different parts of the painting. The doorway is painted with vertical strokes of grey/brown paint, while the sheet is defined by broader, more-or-less horizontal strokes of off-white. The stippling of the wall was created by pushing the paintbrush, holding a grey paint, onto a layer of cream coloured paint, so that the hairs spread out, leaving the grey pattern through which the cream paint is still visible. The overall form of the dog was laid down using long, broad curving strokes of a creamy-brown paint. Shorter strokes of grey show the changes in colour and lustre of the coat – a similar technique was used on the dress.

DAVID HOCKNEY

David Hockney was famous by his mid-twenties, and throughout his career has experimented with different media. As well as painting, he has worked with photography, printmaking and theatre design. He has also used new technologies, such as colour laser copiers and fax machines to create his art.

> *If you want to paint anything worthwhile you shouldn't be afraid of stepping up the pressure.* DAVID HOCKNEY

Hockney was born in Bradford, UK, in 1937, and studied at the Bradford School of Art and the Royal College of Art in London. He was already fairly well known by the time he graduated in 1962 – he had been included in a 1961 exhibition called *Young Contemporaries*. In 1963 he had his first one-man show, and in the same year he visited Los Angeles for the first time. The climate and lifestyle suited him so well that he settled there more or less permanently in 1976. It became a big influence on his work, and he often draws on his experiences in the United States, and particularly the lifestyle of West Coast America.

A Bigger Splash

The title of the painting, *A Bigger Splash* (1967), relates to two other paintings – *The Little Splash* and *The Splash* – all of which were based on a photograph Hockney found in a book about building swimming pools, which he had bought in Hollywood. Hockney described painting all three:

> *The little painting was painted quite quickly, probably in two days. And I thought, it's worth making this bigger, doing it a little differently, and so I did a slightly bigger one,* The Splash, *and I took a bit more care with it. But then I thought the background was perhaps slightly fussy, the buildings were a little too complicated, not quite right. So I decided I'd do a third version, a big one using a very simple building and strong light.* DAVID HOCKNEY

The main elements of the **composition** are the horizontals – the sky, the building, the poolside patio and the pool itself. At the top of the painting there are also the verticals of the building, its windows and the trees. The only strong diagonal is the diving board, which leads your eye into the painting. Without the trees and grass the geometrical composition could almost make this an **abstract** work – even the person who has dived into the pool has disappeared from view, hidden by the splash and the depth of the water.

Technique

A Bigger Splash is painted on a white canvas. Hockney left a large, unpainted border around the edge of the painting, which adds to the flat, geometrical feel of the work. The white line at the top edge of the pool is also unpainted – the colour of the canvas is being used within the painting itself. Hockney divided off the different areas of the painting with masking tape, as he wanted very sharp lines that would help to give an effect of very bright sunlight. Hockney has said he was trying to depict the 'strong Californian light' with its 'bold colour' and 'blue sky' – it was this, after all, which had attracted him to live there.

The masking tape allowed Hockney to paint the main areas of the sky, the building and the pool quickly, applying two or three layers of paint with a roller to create flat, intense surfaces. The only places where colours lie on top of one another are the details applied with a small **sable** brush – the chair, the leaves and the splash itself. The splash is the thickest part of the painting, being built-up from four or five different colours in a series of wavy lines and tiny dots. Hockney has said that it took about two weeks to paint the splash – compared to the two seconds for which the splash itself would have lasted. Instead of the oil paints he had been using in England, for his American works he preferred **acrylic**. 'All this time I was using acrylic paint; texture interested me very little… When you use simple and bold colours acrylic is a fine **medium**; the colours are very intense and they stay intense, they don't alter much.'

Artist and film star

A Bigger Splash was also the title of a film about Hockney made by Jack Hazan in 1974. The film's success in the cinema brought Hockney's work to a wider audience, and helped to increase his fame.

A devoted son?

Hockney had painted his first swimming pool in 1964, and after making a series of images out of handmade paper in 1978 – *The Paper Pools* – he wrote, 'Now I'm going to paint all about figures; I'm not going to paint about swimming pools; I've done enough now.' By this stage though, he had already painted *My Parents* (opposite).

Influences

Hockney gives away some of his influences in *My Parents*. On the shelf in between his parents' legs there is a book about Jean-Siméon Chardin, an 18th century French artist who specialized in interior scenes and **still life** paintings. Indeed, Hockney portrays his parents almost like objects in a still life. His mother, upright and in blue, is like the vase, while his father, at an angle and in brown, is more like the mirror – and like the mirror he is also more 'reflective', looking at a book called *Art and Photography*. On the shelf is a series of books, *Remembrance of Things Past*, by the French author Marcel Proust, which suggests Hockney was thinking about the role of his parents in his upbringing. Reflected in the mirror is a postcard, from the National Gallery in London, of Piero della Francesca's *The Baptism of Christ* – another influence – although he often acknowledges debts to other artists. When writing about *A Bigger Splash*, for example, he referred to Leonardo da Vinci, who made many studies of water.

My parents *(1977). The immobile poses Hockney's mother and father adopt make them look like elements in a still life painting.*

New ideas

Hockney's interest in other artists led him to think about how they worked. In 2002 he wrote a book called *Secret Knowledge* in which he suggested that many artists had used mechanical tools – including lenses and mirrors – to help them paint realistically. However, this might suggest that some artists could not draw well – which we know from their work is not true.

Howard Hodgkin's paintings look unmistakably **abstract** – they are richly coloured and made up of a variety of different shapes, lines and textures. However, according to Hodgkin himself, he is not an abstract artist.

Born in London in 1932, he studied at Camberwell Art School in London, and Bath Academy of Art. It was some time until he gained widespread recognition. In 1984 he was chosen to represent Britain at the Venice **Biennale**, and the following year, partly as a result of his exhibition in Venice, became the second artist to receive the **Turner Prize**. In 1992 he was knighted and became Sir Howard Hodgkin.

Early work

Hodgkin's earliest paintings were more or less realistic – the situation described was easily recognizable. But gradually the realistic elements became less important than the layers of colour and line, which he says are the equivalents of the personal memories on which each work is based.

Dinner at Smith Square

Dinner at Smith Square (1975–79) was painted over a period of four years, and its history can be seen by the way it has been built up in layers. One of the last parts of the painting to be completed, and perhaps the most noticeable element of the painting, is the broad green stripe to the left of centre, which is covered in red dots. Red and green are complementary colours, opposite to each other on the colour wheel, which makes this part of the painting particularly striking. Behind this are other broad areas of darker colours, and an orange area with small green dots. At the top is a small mauve rectangle.

The painting has a wooden frame, but this is also covered with thin splotches of dark-grey paint. Hodgkin often frames his paintings in this way – both with a physical frame, and with a painted border. His idea is to protect the painted area in the centre, shielding it from everything that is outside the painting. He says that the more fragile the emotion that he is trying to depict, 'the more it's got to be protected from the world'.

A painting of friends

In *Dinner at Smith Square* Hodgkin has been quite explicit about the situation that it records: dinner with two of his friends who are married. He said they were sitting on either side of a table, 'talking to each other below a small painting by Bonnard. The husband is on the left leaning back from the table and his wife sits upright on the other side.'

Even with this explanation it is still hard to see which elements of the painting might be derived from the husband, and which from the wife. The small mauve rectangle may be the Bonnard painting, though. After the couple learned that Hodgkin was working on the painting, they regularly invited him back for dinner, and even posed for him so he could sketch their positions. This is possibly the only time that Hodgkin has worked in this way: he usually relies solely on his memory.

Technique

Hodgkin's paintings start their life when a particular event or situation inspires him. From that point he has two ways of working: 'I very often begin a painting by making a reasonably realistic drawing on the panel itself, and then the substitution… of forms and colours for the **representational** drawing begins to take place. But I don't necessarily work like that. I have almost always, in parallel with that method, started by putting down simply a patch of colour'.

Whichever method he uses, the paintings always progress slowly – both *Dinner at Smith Square* and *Dinner in Palazzo Albrizzi* took four years, for example. Hodgkin paints on wood, preferring the hard surface to the 'give' of canvas, and uses oil paint. He wants each individual mark or brush stroke to be important in its own right, and uses a **medium** which is relatively quick-drying so that each layer has dried before the next is applied.

The paint is applied in a number of ways, and often with thick brushes in bold strokes. Two or more colours of paint can be partially mixed together, so that as the brush is pulled across the panel it makes streaks of different colours and tones, showing the direction and movement of the brush stroke. Hodgkin also uses more thinly-loaded brushes, to create feathery strokes, as well as a variety of blobs, dots, splodges and dashes. He carefully builds up the painting layer by layer, gradually adding to, correcting and improving the appearance until he is happy that the painting expresses the memories or emotions he wants to convey.

Dinner in Palazzo Albrizzi

In some cases, Hodgkin may not be entirely happy with the final result. For example *Dinner in Palazzo Albrizzi* was first exhibited in London in August and September 1988, but by the time it was shown in New York in October 1988 he had reworked the painting slightly.

Palazzo Albrizzi is a palace in Venice – Hodgkin was invited to dinner there while he was at the Biennale in 1984. The rich colours, with the green verticals, pink 's-shape' and swirl of blue and white dots suggest this was a more fantastic setting than the comfortable homely feel of *Dinner at Smith Square*.

> *I am in fact a representational painter, though not a painter of appearances. I paint representational pictures of emotional situations. They are equivalents of memories, they stand in for memories of direct experience.* HOWARD HODGKIN

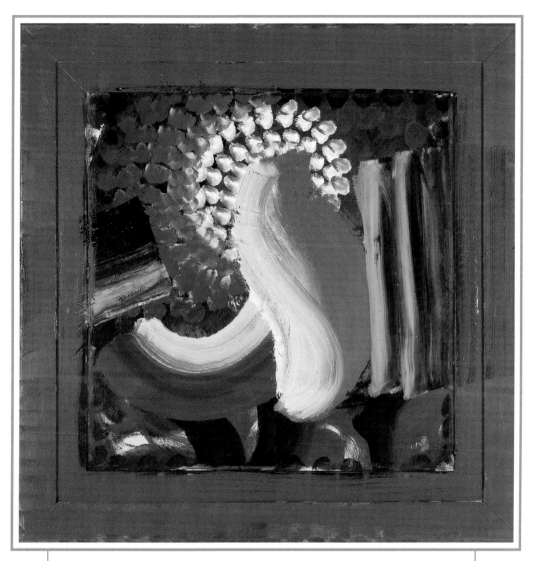

Dinner at Palazzo Abrizzi *(1984–88), Modern Art Museum of Fort Worth. Perhaps the bold painted frame suggests that the emotion Hodgkin depicts here is relatively fragile.*

Influences

Pierre Bonnard (1867–1947), the French artist whose work was part of the inspiration for *Dinner at Smith Square*, is one of Hodgkin's major influences. Like Hodgkin, Bonnard's works often feature interior scenes of people – usually close family and friends – engaged in their everyday activities. However, he often chooses an unusual point of view and, despite being representational, the combination of colour and light is often used to 'abstract' effect.

ALANA JELINEK

Alana Jelinek uses a traditional painting technique – oil on canvas – but the way she displays her work makes it completely different. She uses the realistic appearance of the painting to attract people's attention.

> *What I want to communicate with everything that I do is a kind of questioning about the world. I want to seduce people into questioning the things that they take for granted.* ALANA JELINEK

Jelinek was born in Melbourne, Australia in 1968 and studied Painting at Victoria College, Prahran. In 1991 she moved to London, and completed a Master's degree in Gender, Society and Culture at Birkbeck College in 1994. These issues, particularly the differences between societies and cultures, have always been the focus of her work.

A lot of her art is concerned with tourism and the way in which people travelling from one place to another respond to other cultures, even within their own country. Being Australian she naturally turned to Uluru (Ayers Rock). In her own words, 'It's the place that every Australian vows they will see before they die and will probably never get to. It symbolizes a kind of Australia which actually isn't true.'

Ayers Rock (Uluru)

Ayers Rock (Uluru) (1999) is a very large **un-stretched** canvas, 3.66 metres wide and 12.19 metres long, which is laid on the floor like a carpet. It shows a birds-eye view of a section of Uluru with a line of tourists climbing over it, some of them holding on to the railings which have been inserted into it. For the Aboriginal people of Australia the rock is a very holy site. Their name for it, Uluru, is now the official name, and at the bottom of the rock there is a sign reminding tourists that for Aboriginal people the rock is sacred, and saying they would prefer it if visitors did not walk on it. Nevertheless people still continue to climb the rock. Jelinek is showing us how easily we are prepared to ignore other people's point of view. It was thinking about this that inspired her to display a painting on the floor.

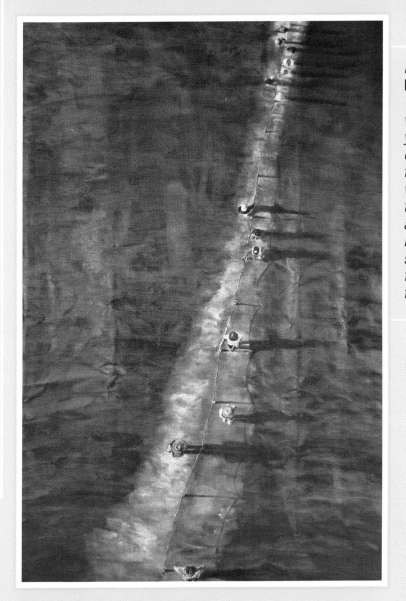

Detail of Ayers Rock (Uluru). *The birds-eye view means that you look down on the hats the tourists are wearing, and so their shadows are more important in showing the figures beneath the hats.*

Taking painting off the wall

While paintings are usually framed and hung on the wall, Jelinek has deliberately treated this one in what, for a painting, might be considered a 'disrespectful' way. Because the famous **Old Master** painters worked with oil on canvas the technique is highly respected, and makes a painting seem valuable.

The canvas took up most of the floor space when it was exhibited, and was designed for the room in which it was exhibited – *Ayers Rock (Uluru)* was a **site-specific installation**. Jelinek made sure there was just enough room for people to get round the edge of the painting without treading or 'trespassing' on it in the way tourists effectively trespass on Uluru itself.

29

On this subject Jelinek says: 'The idea of laying this inherently valuable thing, this massive piece of oil on canvas on the floor, that's almost trespass in the first place, in the way that we normally value things. But then the subject is about trespass, about actually stepping on sacred objects rather than just a piece of oil on canvas. I was playing with the idea of value.'

The birds-eye view was inspired by traditional Aboriginal art, which usually depicts the world as seen from above. Jelinek also says that it is something she started doing after moving into the 22nd floor of a tower block, and looked down on the world around her every day. When the work was painted, she had not visited Uluru, but used photographs and imagined what the birds-eye view would be.

The size of the canvas lying on the floor forces viewers to skirt round the edge of the room, so they do not tread on it.

Unusual methods

Because the painting is so large, Jelinek had to plan it carefully and there were several preparatory studies. The first was relatively small, measuring only 38 cm x 76 cm. It was painted on a door from a kitchen cabinet that she bought in a DIY store.

This small study was scaled up to make a medium-sized work, but this did not have the right proportions for the room in which the work was going to be displayed, so Jelinek made another small-scale sketch. This was used as the basis for the final work, and was scaled up by eye. The canvas was too big to spread out on the floor of her studio, so she attached it to the wall, and painted it standing on a ladder.

Ambushing the audience

As well as exhibiting *Ayers Rock (Uluru)* on the floor Jelinek has also exhibited paintings outside. She says 'I want to ambush my viewers who aren't expecting to see art'. Her earlier works were standard paintings hung on the wall, often featuring people in unusual settings. In one of these, *The Spectators*, a group of tourists on Uluru are apparently taking photographs of anyone looking at the painting. It makes you think about the way tourists look at things, and whether you would like tourists to come and stare at you.

Jelinek realised that she did not have to paint the 'unusual setting' – the setting could be the place in which the work was exhibited. She developed *The Spectators* into a series of life-size cut-out figures, painted on canvas stuck on to MDF. In April 2001 one of the figures was left in the Pilbara Region of the Australian outback. It is called *Shooting the Natives* – a pun, as the man is taking a photograph. It is such a remote place that Jelinek suspects that it may never be seen again.

Influences

Jelinek's early works were heavily influenced by **Surrealism**. The Surrealist interest in the clash of ideas, and placing normal things in unusual settings, is still very much part of her work. She also greatly admires 'those amazing women who came to prominence in the 70s and 80s', including Mary Kelly, Jenny Holzer, Adrian Piper and Susan Hiller.

One of Jelinek's series of paintings called The Spectators. *This particular painting,* Shooting the Natives *(2001), is shown in Australia's outback.*

CHRIS OFILI

When Chris Ofili was awarded the **Turner Prize** in 1998 he was not only the first painter to have won the competition since Howard Hodgkin in 1985, but also the first black artist to win ever. Nevertheless it was not this, but rather his choice of unconventional materials which grabbed the headlines.

> *In the end, I'm trying to bring something up out of the rubble that's pleasing to look at. And I don't know, it might not necessarily make you think of good things, but at least it stimulates your thought.* CHRIS OFILI

Ofili was born in Manchester in the UK in 1968, and studied at the Chelsea School of Art in London. He had his first solo exhibition when he graduated in 1991, before going on to do an MA in Fine Art at the Royal College of Art in London. A British Council travel scholarship in 1992 allowed him to go to Zimbabwe for eight weeks: his parents came from Nigeria, and he wanted to explore his African roots.

Inspiration from Africa

In Zimbabwe Ofili encountered two things which were to have a huge effect on his technique – ancient cave paintings, which inspired the carpet of dots which cover the surfaces of his work, and elephant dung. He liked the idea of using something 'so much a part of the earth in a man-made painting'. As the dung comes from Africa, it can be seen as a reference to Ofili's cultural heritage, although he also liked it simply for its shape and appearance. In the middle of the gorgeously coloured and shiny surfaces it makes us ask questions about the nature of beauty: different things are beautiful in different ways.

No Woman No Cry

No Woman No Cry (1998) is a large painting – 2.44 metres tall and 1.83 metres wide – made higher by the fact that it stands on two balls of varnished elephant dung, with the top of the painting leaning back against the wall. It shows a stunning woman, with bright red lipstick and a richly multicoloured dress, built up of a multitude of swirling, jewel-like dots of paint. She has a necklace made of one of Ofili's hallmark pieces of dung. Her eyes are closed, and she is crying. Embedded within each blue tear is a picture cut from a magazine of a young black man – Stephen Lawrence – murdered in a racist attack in London in 1993. This painting is both a tribute and a memorial to him. The title is taken from a song by Bob Marley released in 1974.

Ofili explains what inspired him to paint this work: 'The image that would always come up in my mind about Stephen Lawrence was the image of his mother crying. But the painting is not a portrait of Doreen Lawrence. It's a meditation on *No Woman No Cry*, which was written, by coincidence, the same year that Stephen Lawrence was born. It still hurts when you see someone crying, and you feel that you have to ask what's wrong or if you can do something to help.'

No Woman No Cry, *lit by ultra-violet light. In the dark or when lit up, the background of the painting glows, and this inscription becomes visible.*

The background, sparkling with glitter, is covered by a diagonal grid made out of small psychedelic circles, like tiny Bridget Riley paintings (see page 48) cut out of paper, which can also be seen through the central image. And if the lights are turned out there is a surprise – in the dark the background glows faintly, and there is a large glowing inscription: 'RIP Stephen Lawrence 22–4–1993'.

Technique

No Woman No Cry was built-up in many layers. The canvas was first covered in a layer of pale yellow-green paint – it is this layer that glows in the dark. The design was first drawn on to the background in pencil: an intricate network of lines can still be seen through all the subsequent layers. Next Ofili stuck down the collage elements – the images of Stephen Lawrence and the 'psychedelic' circles – and then painted the black hearts with **acrylic**. The phosphorescent paint was used again for the inscription, and the elephant dung, which had already been dried and sealed, was attached with a hot glue gun. Polyester resin was poured on to the painting, cementing the dung on to the surface. The glitter was sprinkled on to the resin before it dried. The dark brown outlines were applied with oil paint, and filled in with tiny dots of paint, painstakingly applied over the whole figure.

Preparation

When developing his large scale paintings, Ofili often uses **watercolour**. The one shown here is from a series of 30, all of which show black women with a variety of elaborate hairstyles and bright and colourful costumes. Watercolour is fairly transparent, and the colour of the paper (here it is white) and the initial drawings can be seen through it in the same way that you can see through the overlapping layers of the large-scale paintings. The purples, blues and browns were either painted very wet, or water was added after they were painted to make the colours spread or 'bleed' into one another, creating the rich, swirling appearance of the dress.

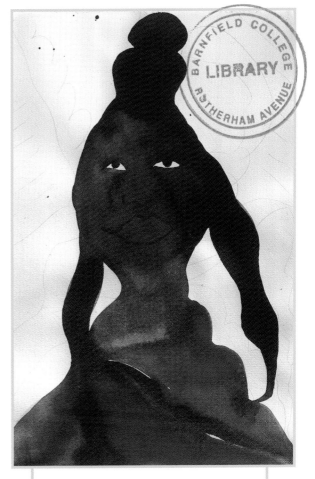

Untitled *(1998), watercolour. This is just one of 30 images that go together to make one work of art.*

Influences

Ofili draws his ideas from the black cultural experience, with sources including **blaxploitation** films and **gangsta rap**. People have compared the way he builds-up his paintings with many layers and collaged elements with the overlapping sounds and samples in contemporary **hip-hop** tracks.

Modern artists who interest him include Bridget Riley, about whom he has said, 'She's like a diva, man. I mean in terms of picture making. That stuff from back in the sixties is still useful.' And a recent work, an **installation** entitled *The Upper Room*, included twelve paintings based on a drawing of a monkey by Andy Warhol.

Ofili's work continues to attract attention. After the outcry some of his works created in the USA, an episode of *The Simpsons* started with Bart Simpson writing on the blackboard, 'I will not create art from dung.' Ofili's work is highly respected, and he was chosen to represent Britain at the Venice **Biennale** in 2003.

ANA MARIA PACHECO

Although Ana Maria Pacheco thinks of herself primarily as a sculptor, painting is very important to her, particularly when it allows her to show something that would not normally be possible.

> *To convey the world of the imagination in painting is less difficult – if you want to hang a figure in mid-air you can put it there and it can be very convincing.* ANA MARIA PACHECO

Pacheco was born in Brazil in 1943, and studied Sculpture at the University of Goiás. After further studies in Music and Education, she started to teach. A British Council Scholarship to the Slade School of Fine Art brought her to London in 1973, and she has lived in England ever since. In 1997 she became the fourth Associate Artist at the National Gallery in London, the first non-European artist, and the first sculptor, to hold the position.

Queen of Sheba and King Solomon in the Garden of Earthly Delights

Queen of Sheba and King Solomon in the Garden of Earthly Delights (1999) is one of the works that Pacheco painted as Associate Artist of the National Gallery. The painting is actually made up of four pictures. Underneath the main image is a strip of smaller paintings, called a predella, inspired by altarpieces that the artist had seen in the National Gallery.

'It would never have occurred to me to make a predella if I had not been at the National Gallery. There is something attractive about having a **narrative** below the main image. The predella panels can be time-based, like a film. I have not placed them in linear sequence, as I like to see them as representations of her [the Queen of Sheba's] dreams.'

Inspiration

The story of the Queen of Sheba comes from the Bible, and is taken up in a number of folk tales. Pacheco drew on these, and her own rich imagination, to create this work. In the main panel we see the Queen of Sheba, a beautiful black woman, in the garden of King Solomon who she has come to visit. The painting is full of references to paintings in the National Gallery, and even the hedge is inspired by a real hedge outside the gallery. The title itself refers to a painting by Hieronymous Bosch (1453–1516) called *The Garden of Earthly Delights*. Pacheco used it because she thought that working in the National Gallery, 'was like being in paradise, it was the Garden of Earthly Delights'.

Details

The Queen of Sheba is stepping on the tail of the peacock, which is often used to represent vanity – maybe she is trying not to be vain. But she is also connected to the deer – it is white like her dress, and the shapes flow into one another. According to Pacheco it may represent the better side of her. Solomon and the monkey also go together – they are painted in similar colours and have similar shifty expressions. Monkeys are often used in paintings to point out how foolish people can be. At the top of the painting is a bird called a hoopoe, which is Solomon's messenger: it can also be seen in the predella carrying the King's invitation to the sleeping Queen. It is placed at the corner of the hedge to make it stand out clearly, although the artist also thinks that putting it in this position helped to make the whole **composition** work.

While she has reason for including all of the details, Pacheco does not necessarily know what all of them 'mean', nor does she think that they need to mean only one thing: 'I like the onlooker to be free to read and interpret the work on their own terms, and in that sense there will be various meanings… I don't want to say what it means, it closes the work.'

This pastel sketch was one of the preliminary studies for the predella of Queen of Sheba and King Solomon in the Garden of Earthly Delights. *It shows the Queen with the head of an evil king.*

Technique

Pacheco's painting technique is one that she has developed herself, using elements from older techniques. Pacheco says she is interested in, 'the light going through the colour. To do that I have to use a lot of transparent colours, and to use that I have to use **gesso**, and to use gesso I have to use wood. That's why I do this.'

The wooden support is first primed and sanded smooth. Pacheco then applies layers of white gesso, sanding them down after every five layers, up to a thickness of about twenty layers. This makes a wonderfully smooth surface on which to paint. She uses oil paint, which allows light to pass through each layer and reflect off the layers underneath. The paint is applied with dollies, bundles of tightly wrapped material, which do not leave any surface textures or brush strokes – Pacheco prefers the surface to be absolutely flat. Unlike many modern artists (starting with the Impressionists), Pacheco does not want there to be any traces of her craftsmanship, because she wants, 'to get the spectator into a world of imagination without any preoccupation of surface or technique.'

When the painting is finished and dry the surface is smoothed down with a very fine glass paper, and then waxed with pure bleached beeswax. Varnish is often used to protect paintings, but this would reflect too much light. The beeswax gives a richness and intensity to the paint.

Old Master paintings were made in natural daylight, and so museums prefer to light them naturally. Pacheco, on the other hand, prefers strong artificial lighting – this will go through the layers of paint, reflecting off the gesso underneath, and brings her colours to life.

Influences

Pacheco has been influenced by many forms of art, from the Folk Art of her native Brazil to artists who she particularly likes, such as Rembrandt van Rijn (1606–69), the most important Dutch artist of the 17th century, the 18th–19th century Spanish artist Franciso de Goya (1746–1828) and Pablo Picasso. Like her, they all worked in printmaking, as well as painting. This, she says, requires you to think about your ideas in advance and work through a process in a set sequence, a discipline that is invaluable when painting. Pacheco's influences are not just found in the visual arts: she is also constantly inspired by music.

JACKSON POLLOCK

Jackson Pollock started his career as a promising, but maybe not outstanding, artist. However in his mid-thirties he developed a new technique which not only revolutionized painting, but also changed the way we think about art. His paintings started from the movements of his own body rather than from conscious thought, and these basic impulses were used and adapted to create the finished work of art.

> When I am in my painting, I'm not aware of what I'm doing. It is only after a sort of 'get acquainted' period that I see what I have been about. I have no fears about making changes, destroying the image, etc., because the image has a life of its own. JACKSON POLLOCK

Pollock was born in Wyoming, USA in 1912, and he had an unstable childhood, as the family moved on a regular basis. In 1928 he went to the Manual Arts High School in Los Angeles, and two years later he travelled to New York to go to the Art Students' League. Pollock's work started to become known when he was part of a group exhibition in New York in 1942, and he had his first solo show the following year.

Within a few years he developed the technique for which he became famous. By 1947 he was no longer applying paint in the traditional way, but by fixing an **un-stretched** canvas to the floor and dripping or pouring the paint on to it. He died less than ten years later, killed when drunk driving at the age of 44.

Reflection of the Big Dipper

Reflection of the Big Dipper (1947) is one of Pollock's most richly coloured works. It has large areas of deep blue and bright yellow, patches of oranges and greens and an intricate tracery of black lines, long white dashes, and red drips and splashes. The overlapping layers of colour and line create a sense of deep and distant spaces. It is almost as if we are looking up at the night sky – or into a reflection of the stars in a pond or lake: the 'Big Dipper' is the name Americans give to the constellation the 'Great Bear', also known as the 'Plough'.

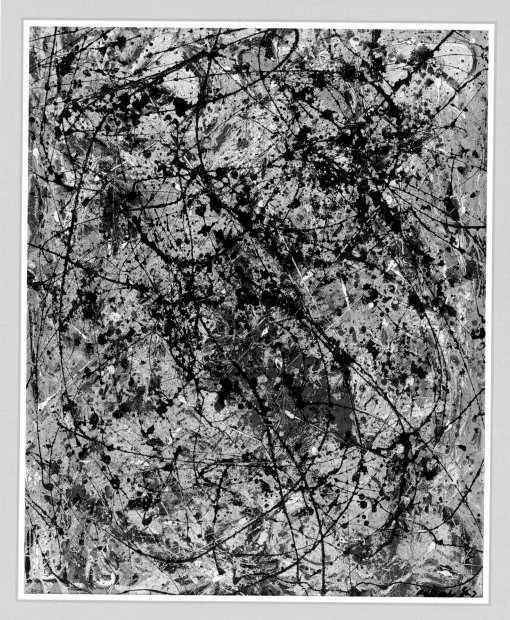

Technique

The canvas was first painted – using a brush – with a layer of pale lilac-grey paint. In places the blues and whites which are part of the mix are less blended than others. The first colour to be added to this would have been the yellow. Although the way it has flowed suggests it was a thin paint, it has not poured down the canvas. This tells us that, like the majority of Pollock's mature work, this was painted on the floor. The lilac paint was still wet when the yellow was applied, and the colours have blended together in parts. The small areas of oranges and greens were added next, followed by the large areas of rich blue, which were poured on to the canvas.

Pollock used a wide variety of tools with which to apply the paint, and as well as brushes used sticks, trowels and knives from which to drip the paint. In some cases he may not have used any implements at all. The white paint in *Reflection of the Big Dipper* (and in some other paintings) can be seen as long, straight lines with a small blob at the end, like elongated white tadpoles. These could have been made by a very rapid flick of a stick or brush loaded with white paint. Alternatively, it has been suggested Pollock might have done this by holding the tube of paint in one hand and banging down hard with the other to 'shoot' the paint across the canvas.

There are some red splashes over the white, suggesting this was added next, dripped and trickled more delicately from a brush or stick. The last paint to be applied was the black. Pollock often used black to 'draw' with. Long looping curves suggest a relatively thin paint and fast, fluid movements.

As well as using brushes, sticks and knives, at times Pollock just poured paint on to the canvas with his hands.

Unique

Each of Pollock's paintings is different, and gains its character from the type and colour of paint used, the way in which it is poured or dripped, and the speed and type of movement that he adopted to apply it. Although we have photographs and even film of Pollock at work, surprisingly little is known about precisely how he made individual paintings. Our evidence must come from looking at the layering of the different colours and the way in which the paint has behaved.

The appearance of the painting could also be affected by varying the materials: as well as standard artists' materials he also used household paints designed for home decoration. Some works also include other substances, such as sand, broken glass and in one case, a key and cigarette butts.

Influences

Pollock liked the work of Picasso, and was particularly drawn to the energy of his painting style. The **Surrealist** artists, interested in the **subconscious**, developed the technique of **automatic drawing**, which relies on the artist making a mark without thinking. This is one possible source for the development of his drip technique. David Alfred Siqueiros, with whom Pollock worked as a student in 1936, had also experimented with different methods of applying paint, including dripping and pouring. According to Pollock himself the technique was, '… akin to the Indian sand painters of the West'. In 1941 he had seen a demonstration by some Navajo artists (they would now be described as Native American rather than Indian) who create imagery by trickling different coloured sands on to the floor.

The impact of Pollock's work

Pollock's painting technique has been described as the most important development in 20th century painting. It challenges the idea that painting is the application of paint to a surface using a tool, and opens it out to a number of different ideas. What we see is a record of the artist's movement – as he moves faster the lines are thinner, if he moves more slowly the lines are thicker, he can make smooth, continuous movements or jerky, angular ones. It was not long before an artist's gestures – the process of making the art – became more important than the finished product, and an audience was invited to see this happen, a type of art known simply as **Performance**.

PAULA REGO

Paula Rego became widely known when she had her first solo show in London at the Serpentine Gallery in 1988. Her work seemed unusual: not only was it **figurative**, but it was also strongly concerned with **narrative** – a combination almost unheard of for artists at the time.

Rego was born in Lisbon, Portugal, in 1935, and came to England to study at the Slade School of Fine Art in London between 1952 and 1956. In 1976 she settled permanently in England, and in 1990 became the first Associate Artist at the National Gallery in London.

Her inspiration is drawn from a wide number of different sources, from newspaper articles to nursery rhymes. She has fond memories of being told elaborate and imaginative stories as a child, and storytelling plays an important part in her work.

Joseph's Dream

In *Joseph's Dream* (1990) Rego confronts one of her favourite themes: the differing roles of men and women. It shows a man, fast asleep, his right arm flopped down over the side of an armchair, and a woman, sitting on a stool intently painting him. At her feet are some drawings, and there are paintings on the wall. Apart from this the room is more or less empty.

Inspiration

Rego was inspired by *The Vision of St Joseph* (shown on page 47), painted by the French artist Philippe de Champaigne in 1638, which is in the National Gallery in London. It shows Joseph asleep, with his carpentry tools and sandals by his side, and an angel appearing from heaven to tell him that Mary is going to be the mother of Jesus.

> *I wanted to do a girl drawing a man very much, because this role reversal is very interesting. She's getting power from doing this you see. And then I went upstairs and I saw Philippe de Champaigne's picture, which I'd never seen before, and the two things fused in some peculiar manner. That picture is so solid, the angel is so solid, and Saint Joseph is so solid. It's wonderful.*
> PAULA REGO

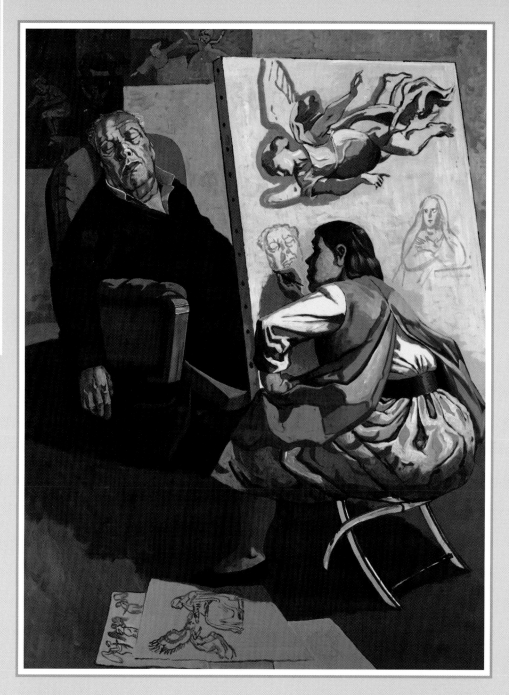

Before the 20th century there were relatively few women painters. The traditional role for women was as the subject of art: they were used as models by male artists. Rego wanted to change this idea by allowing a young girl to make an image of an older man – she has power to do with him what she likes by choosing how to represent him. As we can see above, in Rego's painting it is the woman who does the work, while the man rests.

This sketch, of the head of a sleeping man, was made by Rego in preparation for Joseph's Dream. *In the painting the man is more upright, as if he has been rotated by 90 degrees.*

Details

The painting that the woman is working on looks like a version of Champaigne's. But Rego has used the original painting in other, more subtle ways. Joseph's tools tell us that he is a carpenter. In Rego's version the drawings have the same function, but they do not tell us the business of the sleeping man. Instead, they remind us that it is the woman who has a trade – she is an artist. It is as if the figure of Mary in the background of the original has been brought forward, while Joseph has been moved out of the spotlight to take a less prominent position. The role of the angel is not only repeated in the solid-looking figure that the woman has already painted, but is also referred to by a child looking down from one of the pictures on the wall. These pictures, like the drawings on the floor, are also related to paintings in the National Gallery.

Technique

Like the girl in the painting, Rego started *Joseph's Dream* with a number of sketches on paper, in pencil or pen and ink. Some of these take ideas from Champaigne's original without there being any real visual similarity. In one, for example, the man is stretched out on a bed, rather than a chair, and on the floor are some books and a pair of shoes – an adaptation of the tools and sandals. But there are also studies taken from life, including a drawing of the head and shoulders of a sleeping man: the face was used for the man in the finished painting.

Rego paints on paper that is stuck on to a stretched canvas. She developed this technique as a result of working in **pastels** – many of her works are effectively large-scale drawings, which need to be done on paper. However, *Joseph's Dream* is painted with **acrylic**, which is very smooth to handle, and responds well to the paper. The finished work has a fairly restricted **palette** of blues, browns and whites, although traces of red on the artist's apron suggest Rego changed her mind while painting, covering it with a light blue. This gives a depth and richness to the colour of the apron.

The Vision of St Joseph (*c.1638*), by Philippe de Champaigne, National Gallery (London). Rego was inspired by this painting while working as Associate Artist at the gallery.

Influences

At the age of fourteen Rego was given a book on **Dada** and **Surrealism** by her father, and the Surrealists, especially Max Ernst (1891–1976), have always had a strong influence on her work. As well as other artists, notably Picasso and Jean Dubuffet, she has also been influenced by wider cultural sources, such as the early films of Walt Disney and children's book illustrations. Working at the National Gallery led her to confront the work of the **Old Masters**, reinterpreting the paintings and their stories from a woman's point of view and reminding us how few 'Old Mistresses' there are.

BRIDGET RILEY

Bridget Riley's paintings combine colours and forms to create striking visual effects, using the interaction between the colours themselves to create a sense of movement and energy. Riley was born in 1931, spending most of her childhood in Cornwall, UK. She studied Painting at Goldsmiths College in London and the Royal College of Art also in London. Her first solo exhibition was in 1962.

Early success

The paintings for which she first became famous were in black and white, made up of a repetition of a number of basic units.

Later in the 1960s, Riley started to use colour, as she had noticed that if certain colours were painted next to one another they would create the appearance of additional, fleeting colours.

*In Zig Zag (1961) the strong contrasts and varied spacing of the diagonals make the painting appear to glow and flicker. The paint is **tempera**, its natural smoothness is enhanced by the fact that it was painted on hardboard.*

Influences

The greatest influence on Riley was undoubtedly Georges Seurat, the 19th century artist whose investigation of colour led him to develop **Pointillism**. She is also interested in the work of Peter Paul Rubens (1577–1640), Claude Monet (1840–1926) and Henri Matisse (1869–1954), who she describes, with Seurat, as 'the great masters of colour'.

Entice

Entice (1974) only uses three colours, red, blue and green, combined with the neutral grey and white. The bands of colour cross the entire canvas: the long boundaries between them allow the colours to interact as much as possible. The waving forms create an alternation of wider and narrower bands of colour, which changes the way they interact.

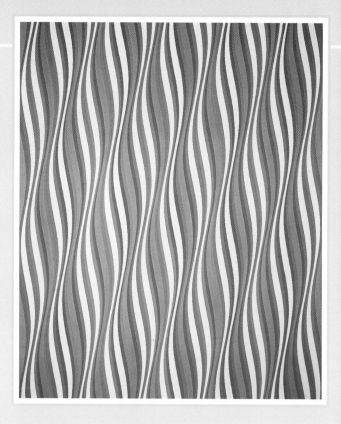

Technique

Riley mixes her own paints, as the effects she wants to achieve are dependent on the precise quality of the paint. She works first in gouache – an opaque water-based paint with the right intensity of colour – to create a series of studies investigating the relationship of particular colours. Riley is not always happy with these studies – sometimes they just do not create an interesting result.

For the studies that do look promising a full-sized **cartoon** is made, again using gouache on paper. This forms the basis for a finished work, painted on canvas, first with **acrylic**, and then with oil paints. All of this is done by hand – she does not use masking tape to stop one colour crossing the other as this can cause ridges at the boundaries. For similar reasons the paintings are executed by her assistants. Riley does not want any individual marks or brush strokes to be seen, as this would interfere with the relationships between the colours. Even if she does not execute her own paintings Riley is solely responsible for their appearance – the colour relationships are her creation, regardless of who actually paints the finished work.

> *I want to bring about a situation in which my work can throw up surprises.* BRIDGET RILEY

TIMELINE

1435 Alberti writes his book *On Painting*

1839 Invention of photography

1873 Claude Monet paints *Impression: Sunrise*, the painting that gave **Impressionism** its name

1881 Pablo Picasso is born

1907 **Cubism** developed

1912 Jackson Pollock is born

1913 Marcel Duchamp creates *Bicycle Wheel*, the first **readymade**, from a bicycle wheel and a wooden stool

1914 Outbreak of World War I

1915 **Dada** is founded in Zurich

1918 End of World War I

1922 Lucian Freud is born in Germany

1924 **Surrealism** is founded in Paris

1931 Bridget Riley is born

1932 Howard Hodgkin is born

1933 Adolf Hitler is elected Chancellor of Germany

The Freud family moves to Britain

1935 Paula Rego is born

1937 David Hockney is born

1939 Outbreak of World War II

1941 Michael Craig-Martin is born

1943 Ana Maria Pacheco is born

1945 End of World War II

1947 Jackson Pollock develops his 'drip' technique

1952 George VI dies: Princess Elizabeth becomes Queen Elizabeth II

1956   Jackson Pollock dies, killed while drink driving

1960   Jean-Michel Basquiat is born

1968   Alana Jelinek and Chris Ofili are born

1973   Pablo Picasso dies
         David Hockney is the subject of the film *A Bigger Splash*

1974   Bob Marley releases the song *No Woman No Cry*
         Stephen Lawrence is born

1984   Howard Hodgkin represents Britain at the Venice **Biennale**

1985   *Uluru* (Ayers rock) is returned to its Aboriginal owners
         Howard Hodgkin awarded the Turner Prize

1987   Jean-Michel Basquiat dies as the result of a drug overdose

1990   Paula Rego becomes the first Associate Artist of the National
         Gallery in London

1992   Hodgkin is knighted, becoming Sir Howard Hodgkin

1993   Stephen Lawrence is murdered

1997   Ana Maria Pacheco becomes Associate Artist at the National
         Gallery in London

1998   Chris Ofili wins the **Turner Prize** – the first black artist to do so

2000   Tate Modern, Britain's collection of 20th and 21st century art, is opened
         in the former Bankside power station in London

2003   Chris Ofili represents Britain at the Venice Biennale

GLOSSARY

abstract work of art which does not reproduce the visual appearance of something, but relies on colour, line, pattern and texture to convey ideas or emotions

acrylic artificial water soluble, quick drying paint medium invented in the 20th century

automatic drawing drawing without thinking. It was a technique used by the Surrealists, who would draw (or scribble) something and then use this subconscious gesture as the basis for a work of art.

Biennale Italian for biennial, something that happens every two years. The Italian is used because one of the most important international biennial art exhibitions takes place in Venice.

blaxploitation short for 'black exploitation', and applied to a type of film made with black actors for a black audience

cartoon drawing or painted study made in preparation for a painting which is the same size as the finished work

composition way in which the elements of a painting are arranged

Conceptual work of art for where ideas are more important than the appearance

Cubism influential artistic style developed in the 1900s in which artists do not reproduce what they see from a single viewpoint, but analyse a subject, depicting different parts of it from different points of view

Dada movement founded in Switzerland in 1915. Artists attacked traditional notions of art, often leaving everything to chance.

figurative paintings showing figures, or recognisable subject matter. This is another word for representational.

gangsta rap rap music with violent and aggressive lyrics

gesso white substance used to prepare a support for painting. The word is derived from the substance gypsum (calcium sulphate) which was commonly used in Italian paintings.

Graffiti Art the brightly coloured decorative words sprayed on walls which became popular as a form of street art in the 1970s and 80s

graphic relating to drawing, or the use of line. Painting can be graphic if the artist is more interested in lines and drawn details than large areas of painterly colour.

hip-hop form of music related to break-dancing, Graffiti Art and a style of dress

impasto thick layer of paint that sticks out from the painting

Impressionism style of painting that developed in France in the 1860s which used colour to create a sense of mood and light, but was not concerned with showing precise details

installation work of art that is put together or 'installed' in a room or space which relies on the space as part of its effect

medium liquid which is mixed with a pigment to make a paint. It must be fluid enough to allow the paint to be applied, but will dry, making sure that the pigment is still attached.

narrative story (a narrative painting is one which illustrates a story)

Old Master artists before the mid-19th century, and especially from the 16th and 17th centuries, for example Rembrandt

painterly achieving the effects of painting. This can be related to the rich use of paint itself, the creation of broad brushstrokes and areas of colour, but the term is also applied to techniques including drawing and photography.

palette range of colours an artist uses. The name comes from the wooden board on which an artist arranges paints, also called a palette.

pastel crayon made of chalk, coloured and mixed with binding material

Performance form of art that developed in the 1960s which relies on an audience to watch the artist performing

pigment coloured substance used to make a paint. Originally pigments would have been a powder made from plant or animal material, or from rocks and minerals. Most are now manufactured.

Pointillism style developed by Georges Seurat in the 1880s which involved applying separate dots (or points) of pure colour to a painting.

primitive from the earliest periods in history

readymade object which already exists which the artist selects and displays in a museum or art gallery to give it the status of art

Renaissance French word meaning 'rebirth', referring to changes in European culture between the late 14th and early 17th centuries

representational work of art that depicts or represents something that can be seen

sable soft brown fur of the sable, a type of animal, which is used to make paintbrushes

site specific work of art made for a particular place or site. Its size, shape, appearance and meaning can be the result of the place it is made for.

still life painting or drawing of a collection of still objects, such as fruit

stipple to engrave, paint or draw with dots rather than lines

stretcher wooden frame around which a canvas is stretched in order to make it firm enough to paint on

subconcious activity of our brain that we are not usually aware of

Surrealism/Surrealists artistic movement which developed from Dada. Surrealists were interested in the world of dreams and the subconscious.

tempera paint made with egg yolk as the medium, favoured in Italian painting up until the 15th century

Turner Prize annual prize given to a British artist under the age of 50 for an outstanding exhibition or other presentation of their work

un-sized canvas which has not been sealed with size. The paint then soaks into the canvas, staining it, rather than remaining on the surface.

un-stretched canvas which has not been attached to a stretcher

watercolour paint using water as the medium, which is more or less transparent

KEY WORKS

JEAN-MICHEL BASQUIAT
Arroz con Pollo, 1981, John Goodman Gallery, New York.
Untitled (Quality), 1983, Whitney Museum of American Art, New York.

MICHAEL CRAIG-MARTIN
An Oak Tree 1973, Tate, UK
Inhale/Exhale 2002, Installation at Manchester Art Gallery

LUCIAN FREUD
Interior in Paddington 1951, Walker Art Gallery, Liverpool
Factory in North London 1972, private collection
Double Portrait 1985-6, private collection

DAVID HOCKNEY
A Bigger Splash 1967, Tate, UK
My Parents 1977, Tate, UK

HOWARD HODGKIN
Dinner at Smith Square 1975-79, Tate, UK
Dinner at Palazzo Abrizzi 1984-88, Modern Art Museum of Fort Worth, Texas
Bedtime 1999-2001, National Museum and Gallery, Cardiff

ALANA JELINEK
Ayers Rock (Uluru) 1999, collection of the artist
Shooting the Natives 2001, Pilbara Region, Western Australia

CHRIS OFILI
No Woman No Cry 1998, Tate, UK
Untitled 1998, Tate (set of 30 watercolours)

JACKSON POLLOCK
Reflection of the Big Dipper 1947, Stedelijk Museum, Amsterdam
Blue Poles: Number 11 1952, National Gallery of Australia, Canberra

ANA MARIA PACHECO
The Endeavours of a Certain Poet 1985, Whitworth Art Gallery, Manchester
Queen of Sheba and King Solomon in the Garden of Earthly Delights 1999, private collection

PAULA REGO
Joseph's Dream 1990, private collection
Crivelli's Garden 1990, National Gallery, London
The Artist in her Studio 1993, Leeds City Art Gallery

BRIDGET RILEY
Zig-Zag 1961, Robert Sandelson Gallery, London
Entice 1974, private collection
Nataraja 1993, Tate, UK

WHERE TO SEE WORKS

Almost all of the artists described have at least one work in the Tate collections. These works could be exhibited in London at Tate Modern or Tate Britain, or at Tate Liverpool or Tate St Ives. The other collections mentioned in the Key Works section on page 54 – in Cardiff, Liverpool, Manchester, Leeds and Canberra (Australia) also include works by several of these artists. If travelling to see a specific work it is always worthwhile checking in advance that the work is on show.

FURTHER READING AND WEB SITES

The Impact of Modern Paints, Jo Crook and Tom Learner (Tate Gallery Publishing 2000)
The Turner Prize, Virginia Button (Tate Gallery Publishing 1999)
Jean-Michel Basquiat, Richard Marshall (Whitney Abrams 1992)
Basquiat, Phoebe Hoban (Quartet Books 1998)
Michael Craig-Martin: Inhale/Exhale, Richard Cork and Virginia Button (Manchester Art Gallery 2002)
Interpreting Lucian Freud, David Alan Mellor (Tate Gallery Publishing 2002)
Hockney on Art, David Hockney (Little, Brown 2002)
That's the way I see it, David Hockney (Thames and Hudson 1999)
Howard Hodgkin, Andrew Graham-Dixon (Thames and Hudson 2001)
Howard Hodgkin Paintings, Michael Auping et al (Thames and Hudson 1997)
Chris Ofili – The Upper Room, Susannah Paisley (Victoria Miro Gallery 2002)
Chris Ofili, Godfrey Worsdale (Serpentine Gallery Trust 1998)
Ana Maria Pacheco in the National Gallery, Kathleen Adler, Colin Wiggins (National Gallery Company Ltd 2000)
Exercise of Power: The Art of Ana Maria Pacheco, George Szirtes (Lund Humphries 2001)
Interpreting Pollock, Jeremy Lewison (Tate Gallery Publishing 2001)
Paula Rego, Fiona Bradley (Tate Gallery Publishing 2002)
The Eye's Mind: Bridget Riley: Collected Writings 1965–1999, Bridget Riley and Robert Kudielka (Thames and Hudson 1999)
Bridget Riley: Selected Paintings, 1961–1999,Michael Krajewski et al (Hatje Cantz 1999)

The following web sites show paintings by the artists mentioned in this book:
www.tate.org.uk
www.artchive.com
www.tate.org.uk/britain/exhibitions/freud/
www.axisartists.org.uk/all/ref2984.htm (for Alana Jelinek)
www.anamariapacheco.co.uk

INDEX